PATRICK MAHOMES

NFL STAR

By Douglas Lynne

Book design by Jake Nordby
Cover design by Jake Nordby

Photographs ©: Steve Sanders/Kansas City Chiefs/AP Images, cover, 1; Paul Spinelli/AP Images, 4, 16, 23; Tyler Kaufman/AP Images, 6–7; David J. Phillip/AP Images, 9; Kathy Willens/AP Images, 10; Victor Texcucano/Tyler Morning Telegraph/AP Images, 13; Tim Warner/Cal Sport Media/AP Images, 14; Ryan Kang/AP Images, 18; Logan Bowles/AP Images, 21; Red Line Editorial, 22

Press Box Books, an imprint of Press Room Editions.

Library of Congress Control Number: 2023909338

ISBN
978-1-63494-760-2 (library bound)
978-1-63494-767-1 (paperback)
978-1-63494-780-0 (epub)
978-1-63494-774-9 (hosted ebook)

Distributed by North Star Editions, Inc.
2297 Waters Drive
Mendota Heights, MN 55120
www.northstareditions.com

Printed in the United States of America
102023

ABOUT THE AUTHOR

Douglas Lynne is a freelance writer. He spent many years working in the media, first in newspapers and later for online organizations, covering everything from breaking news to politics to entertainment to sports. He lives in Minneapolis, Minnesota.

TABLE OF CONTENTS

15
C
LIV
Wilson

CHAMPION QUARTERBACK

1

The Kansas City Chiefs trailed the San Francisco 49ers 20–17. Just 3:45 remained in Super Bowl LIV. It was time for star quarterback Patrick Mahomes to make a difference. The 49ers defense was one of the best in the National Football League (NFL). But Mahomes could make difficult throws against even the toughest opponents.

Mahomes looks for an open receiver while running away from defenders.

Mahomes points out a defender who might rush the quarterback.

Mahomes took the snap on second and seven. His eyes darted around the field. He spotted receiver Sammy Watkins streaking down the right sideline. Mahomes released a

long, looping pass. Watkins caught the ball in stride. He ran all the way to the 11-yard line.

A few plays later, the Chiefs faced third down from the 5-yard line. Mahomes calmly stepped back in the pocket. This time, he used his short-range accuracy to find running back Damien Williams in front of the goal line. Williams barely had time to catch the ball before defenders closed in on him. He quickly spun and dove for the end zone. He crossed the goal line for the go-ahead touchdown. After the extra point, the Chiefs led 24–20.

YOUNG STAR

Patrick Mahomes's incredible performance earned him the Super Bowl Most Valuable Player (MVP) Award. That made him the youngest quarterback ever to win the honor. Mahomes also became the second Black quarterback to win the award. The first was Washington quarterback Doug Williams, who won it after the 1987 season.

The Chiefs added another late touchdown and won Super Bowl LIV. Mahomes became a champion at just 24 years old. And his first Super Bowl trophy wouldn't be his last.

Mahomes celebrates with his teammates after winning Super Bowl LIV.

2

BORN TO PLAY

Patrick Mahomes was born on September 17, 1995, in Tyler, Texas. His father, Pat, was a Major League Baseball (MLB) player. Patrick went to many of his dad's games and watched the athletes in action. Growing up, Patrick spent a lot of time playing baseball. He developed a powerful throwing arm. That also helped him on the football field.

Patrick sometimes warmed up with professional baseball players before their games.

At Whitehouse High School, Patrick's arm was on full display. During his senior year, Patrick threw for 4,619 yards and 50 touchdowns. When it came time for college, Patrick decided to stay close to home. He chose to attend Texas Tech University.

At first, Mahomes played both football and baseball at Texas Tech. But after his freshman season, he decided to give up baseball. He wanted to focus on football. In his sophomore season, Mahomes became the team's starting quarterback.

No matter where his receivers were on the field, Mahomes was accurate. He had the

TWO-SPORT TALENT

Before Patrick Mahomes chose to attend Texas Tech, he was selected in the 2014 MLB Draft. The Detroit Tigers picked him in the 37th round. But Mahomes didn't want to give up football. So, he never signed a contract with the Tigers.

Patrick was named the Texas high school football player of the year in 2013.

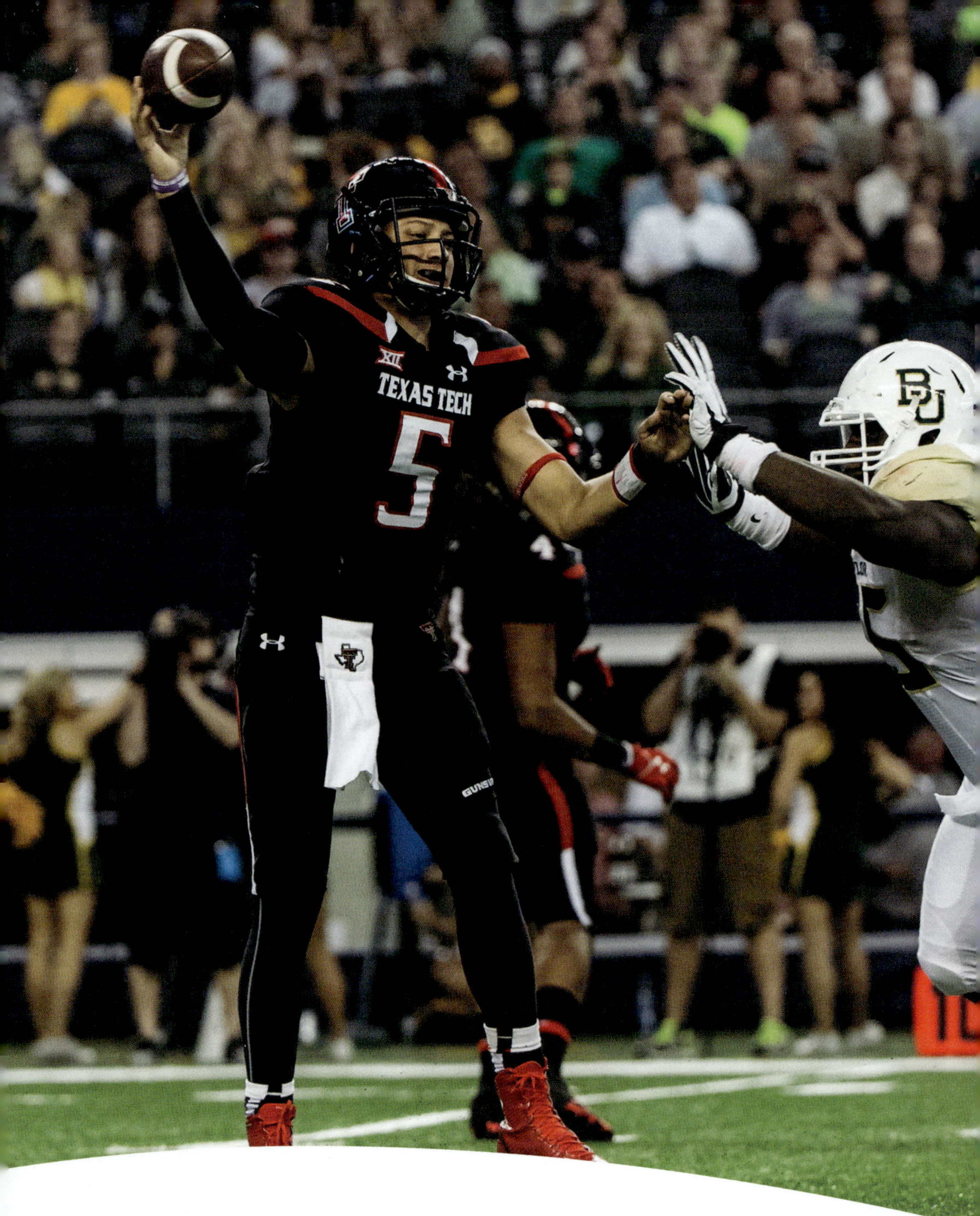

Mahomes was skilled at completing passes even when defenders were about to tackle him.

arm strength to throw deep passes. He was also a threat to run with the ball. In 2015, Mahomes threw for 4,653 yards and 36 touchdowns. He also rushed for 456 yards and 10 touchdowns.

Mahomes only got better in his junior season. After a year of hard work, he became one of college football's superstars. His 5,052 passing yards led all quarterbacks. In a game against Oklahoma, Mahomes recorded an incredible 819 total yards. That was the most ever by a single player in a college football game.

Mahomes caught the attention of NFL scouts. When he announced that he would enter the 2017 NFL Draft, many teams were excited for a chance to sign the rising star.

15
15
adidas

3

THE BIGGEST STAGE

Patrick Mahomes impressed scouts at the 2017 NFL Combine. His passes were clocked at 60 miles per hour. That tied the record for the fastest throw ever recorded at the combine. Teams could tell that Mahomes was a unique player.

The Kansas City Chiefs were one of those teams. They had the 27th overall pick in the 2017 NFL Draft. But they traded up to the 10th spot to select Mahomes.

Mahomes became Kansas City's starting quarterback in his second NFL season.

Mahomes is quick, so defenders have a hard time catching him.

Mahomes served as the Chiefs' backup quarterback in 2017. Starting quarterback Alex Smith taught him valuable lessons about how to succeed in the NFL.

In his second season, Mahomes took over the starting job. He paired his arm talent with creativity and speed in the pocket. Even if defenders had him trapped, Mahomes would often wiggle out of trouble and complete a spectacular pass. His performance earned him the 2018 NFL MVP Award.

In the 2019 season, Mahomes led the Chiefs to their first Super Bowl in decades. And Mahomes put on a show. He led the Chiefs to a comeback win.

15 AND THE MAHOMIES

In 2019, Patrick Mahomes helped set up a group called 15 and the Mahomies. This group teaches the importance of education and children's health. Its main program, 15 FOR 15, supports after-school programs that focus on science, the arts, and athletics.

After that, Mahomes signed a 10-year, $503 million contract with the Chiefs. It was the largest contract in American sports history.

In 2022, Mahomes had another MVP season. More importantly, he led the Chiefs back to the Super Bowl. This time, they faced the Philadelphia Eagles. The Chiefs were down 10 points at halftime. But Mahomes led his team on three straight touchdown drives to open the second half. The Chiefs won 38–35. Mahomes's three touchdown passes earned him another Super Bowl MVP. He became the first NFL player to win both the regular-season MVP and Super Bowl MVP in the same season. Patrick Mahomes proved that he ranked among the NFL's greatest players.

PATRICK MAHOMES
CAREER PASSING STATISTICS

- **2017** – 284 yards, 0 TDs, 1 interception
- **2018** – 5,097 yards, 50 TDs, 12 interceptions
- **2019** – 4,031 yards, 26 TDs, 5 interceptions
- **2020** – 4,740 yards, 38 TDs, 6 interceptions
- **2021** – 4,839 yards, 37 TDs, 13 interceptions
- **2022** – 5,250 yards, 41 TDs, 12 interceptions

Mahomes threw two touchdown passes in the fourth quarter of Super Bowl LVII.

TIMELINE MAP

1. **Tyler, Texas: 1995**
   Patrick Mahomes is born on September 17.
2. **Whitehouse, Texas: 2013**
   Mahomes finishes his prep career at Whitehouse High School, playing both football and baseball.
3. **Lubbock, Texas: 2015**
   Mahomes takes over as Texas Tech's starting quarterback in his sophomore season, and he puts up amazing numbers.
4. **Philadelphia, Pennsylvania: 2017**
   On April 27, Mahomes is selected 10th overall by the Kansas City Chiefs in the NFL Draft.
5. **Denver, Colorado: 2017**
   Mahomes starts his first NFL game, and the Chiefs defeat the Denver Broncos 27–24 on December 31.
6. **Miami, Florida: 2020**
   Mahomes leads the Chiefs to a Super Bowl victory over the San Francisco 49ers on February 2.
7. **Kansas City, Missouri: 2020**
   Mahomes signs a 10-year, $503 million contract with the Chiefs. It's the largest contract in American sports history.
8. **Glendale, Arizona: 2023**
   On February 12, Mahomes wins his second Super Bowl with the Chiefs, this time over the Philadelphia Eagles. Mahomes earns the Super Bowl MVP for the second time.

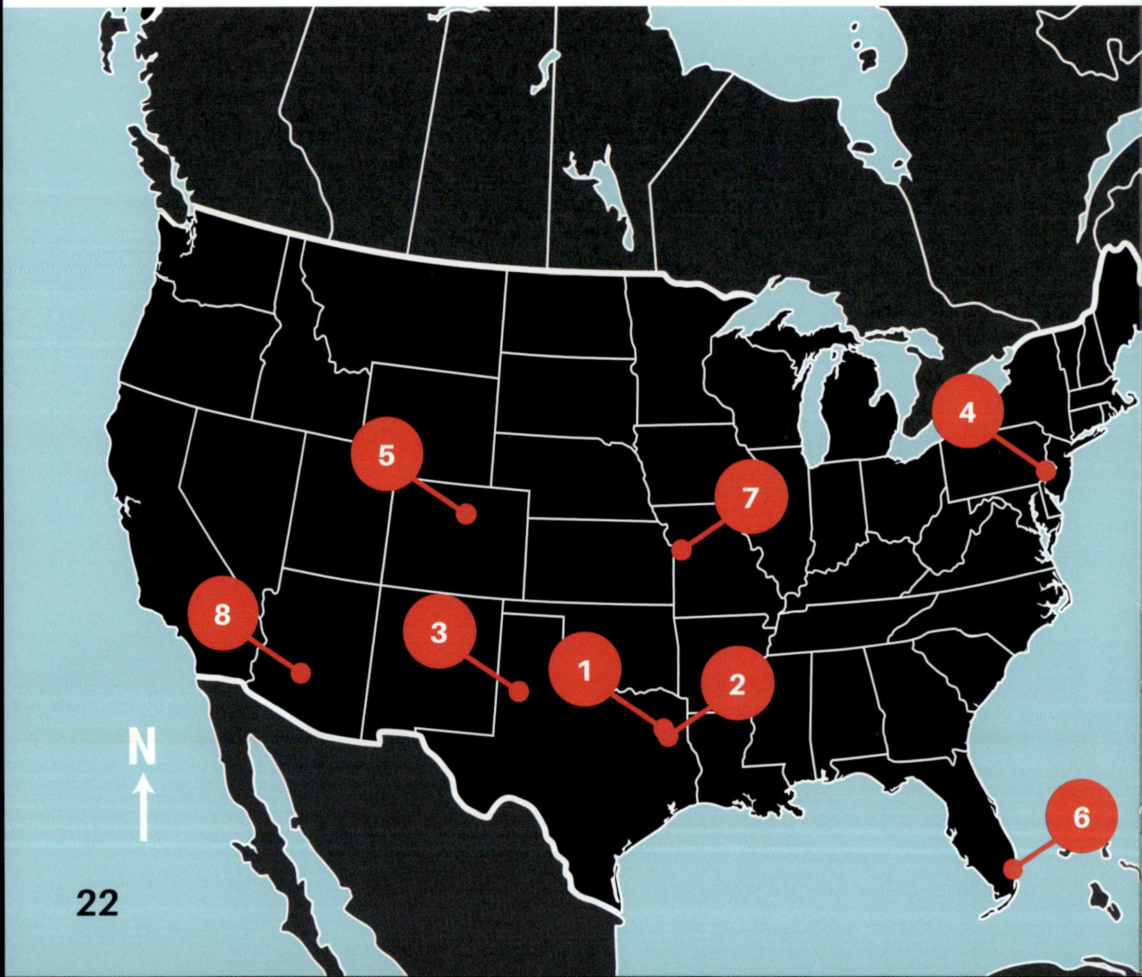

AT-A-GLANCE

PATRICK MAHOMES

Birth date: September 17, 1995

Birthplace: Tyler, Texas

Position: Quarterback

Height: 6 feet 2 inches

Weight: 225 pounds

Current team: Kansas City Chiefs (2017–)

Past team: Texas Tech Red Raiders (2014–16)

Major awards: Second-Team All-Big 12 (2016), Sammy Baugh Trophy (2016), Bert Bell Award (2018), NFL Offensive Player of the Year (2018), Pro Bowl (2018–22), First-Team All-Pro (2018, 2022), NFL MVP (2018, 2022), Super Bowl MVP (2019, 2022), Super Bowl Champion (2019, 2022)

Accurate through the 2022 season.

MORE INFORMATION

To learn more about Patrick Mahomes, go to **pressboxbooks.com/AllAccess**.

These links are routinely monitored and updated to provide the most current information available.

GLOSSARY

accurate
Able to throw a ball directly where the person aims it.

combine
An event before the NFL Draft where college players show their skills.

contract
A signed agreement that states how much a team will pay a player and for how many years.

draft
An event that allows teams to choose new players coming into the league.

pocket
The area behind the line of scrimmage where the quarterback is protected by blockers.

scout
A person who studies players and grades their skills.

INDEX